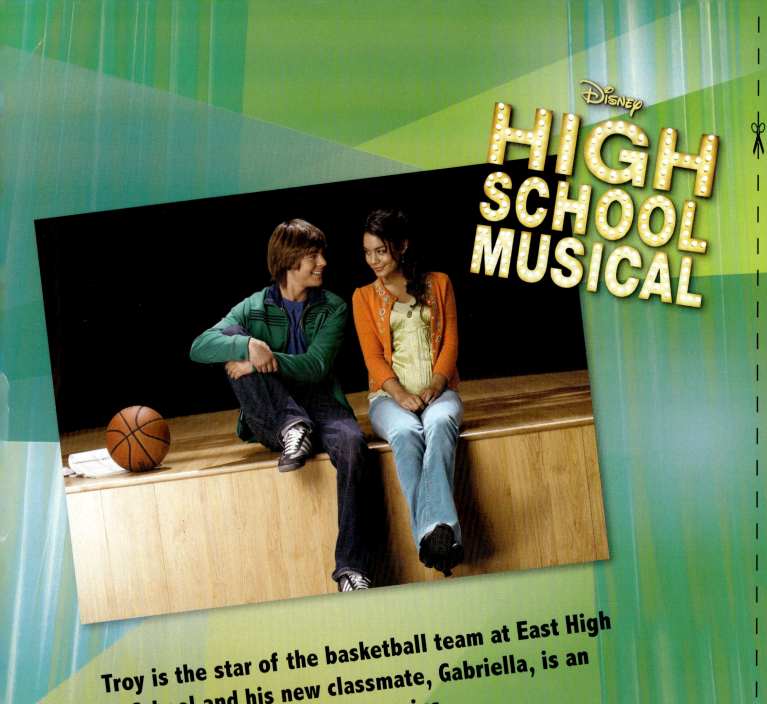

Troy is the star of the basketball team at East High School and his new classmate, Gabriella, is an academic genius.

Troy and Gabriella seem to be from different worlds. When auditions for the school musical begin, singing brings them together to face a huge challenge: to win the starring roles!

TROY BOLTON

ACHIEVEMENTS:
Captain of the East High School Basketball Team.
Starring role in the school musical opposite Gabriella.

BEST FRIEND:
Chad and other members of the
school basketball team.

HOBBIES:
Basketball and singing.

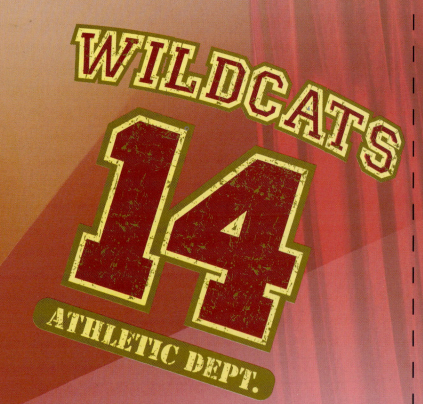

Gabriella Montez

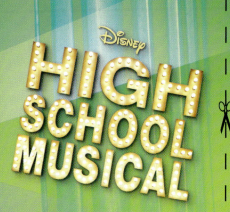

HOBBIES: Anything academic-she loves maths and science! Singing with Troy.

BEST FRIEND: Taylor and other members of the East High Scholastic Decathlon Team.

EMBARRASSING MOMENT: Standing up to sing a solo in church and being too shy to do so!

ACHIEVEMENTS: Winning the Scholastic Decathlon. Getting the lead in the school musical opposite Troy!

SCHOOL RIVAL: Sharpay Evans. Sharpay has starred in seventeen high school musicals. She comes up with a plan to make sure Gabriella doesn't get her part, but her plan fails!

Sharpay Evans

Disney HIGH SCHOOL MUSICAL

KNOWN AS: The Teen Drama Queen.

HOBBIES: Singing and dancing with her brother, Ryan.

BEST FRIEND: Her brother Ryan. Sharpay doesn't need friends. She's a legend in her own mind.

AMBITION: To play the lead in every school musical ever produced! Or to become a star!

ACHIEVEMENTS: Starring in seventeen musical productions at East High School.

SCHOOL RIVAL: Anyone who wants to audition for the lead role in the school musical. Gabriella as she sings so well!

The Teen Drama Queen

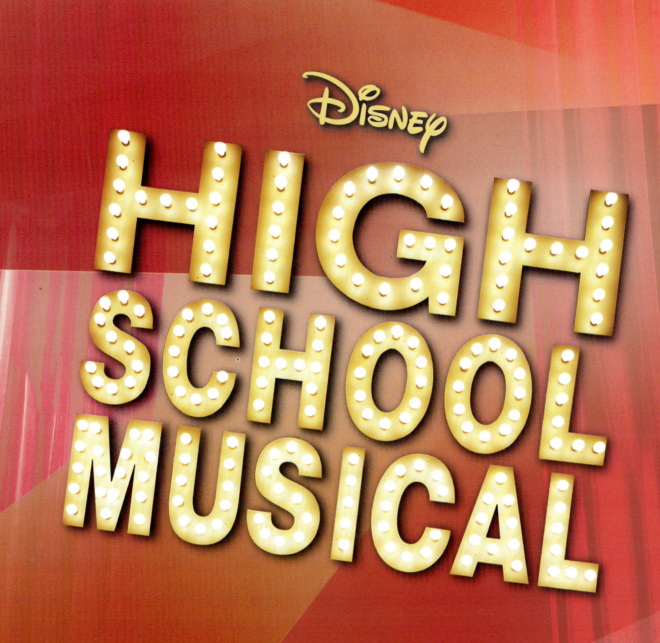

Chad Danforth

Disney HIGH SCHOOL MUSICAL

HOBBIES: Playing basketball and hanging out with the basketball team.

BEST FRIEND: Troy Bolton, the basketball team captain. Chad has a bit of a soft spot for Taylor too!

MAIN FOCUS: To make sure the Wildcats win the basketball championship. He'll do anything to make that happen!

GET'CHA HEAD IN THE GAME